DONUT TO MY BROCCOLY

WRITTEN BY TIMOTHY MCGRATH
ILLUSTRATED BY TARYN PELLI

Siena and Kinsley are in their playroom playing with their dolls, when all of a sudden Kinsley's stomach starts to growl.

"Rrrr,Gurgle,Rrrr"

She rubs her tummy and says "ohh, Siena I think I'm hungry."

Mrs. McGrath the girls mom, asks the girls,

"What would you like to eat girls?"

Kinsley shouts **"Pasta!"**

Siena calmly says,

"How about something healthy, you always want pasta."

Kinsley sighs "but I don't know what's healthy."

Siena leans over and puts her arm around her disappointed sister.

"Don't worry Kins, I'll teach you."

Siena asks Kinsley a few questions...

"What do you like to eat that grows from the earth?"

Kinsley gets excited and claps her hands and smiles ear to ear

and hollers out **"Donuts!"**

Both girls laugh until their bellies hurt.

"No seriously Kins, what about salad, broccoli, or carrots?"

You like all of those things.

Those are vegetables. They grow from the earth like all the vegetables in grandpa's garden. Vegetables are a carbohydrate that give us energy and nutrients to help us grow strong. They help us have the energy to play and ride our bikes. Vegetables fill our muscles with fuel just like putting gas in a car or charging our iPad. They give us the energy we need to have fun and get around.

What are some vegetables you like?

"Broccoli, I like broccoli!"

"Mom, can you make us broccoli?"

"But...in the oven, I like them crispy like chips."

"Sure, would you like anything else with your broccoli?"

Kinsley quickly shouts **"Pasta!"**

Siena starts to giggle "Kinsley, we already said no to pasta,

you always want pasta!"

"You want to learn to eat healthy, right Kins"?

"Yes!" Kinsley screams

"Ok, we'll have a vegetable right Kins?"

"Yes, broccoli."

"Now we need a protein, do you know what a protein is?"

"Yes, donuts."

Everybody in the room starts to laugh again.

"Kinsley, what about chicken, steak or fish?"

"Ewww, I'm not going to eat a fish...that's disgusting!"

"Ok, what about chicken, you like chicken?"

"Yes, chicken, I like chicken. MA, MAAAA can you please make us chicken?"

"But... the chicken that you cut in squares with the special dipping sauce."

"Good Kins, we now have a carbohydrate to give us energy, and chicken as our protein to help our muscles grow and get stronger. They are like all the Lego's we need to build the princess castle. Or all the pieces we need to build a puzzle. Proteins help us build strong healthy muscles."

"Do you think we need to add anything else Kins?"

Kinsley screams again **"Donuts!"**

But she's just being silly as she smiles at her mom and

Siena walks away to go play with her dolls.

While Mrs. McGrath cooks lunch the girls continue to giggle and play.

Siena asks Kinsley, "Did you learn anything about healthy eating today?"

Kinsley using her doll to talk

"YES, I like Broccoli, and……. Hehe giggles" and…"DONUTS"

Both girls laugh and laugh.

Mrs. McGrath yells upstairs "lunch is ready."

The girls run downstairs to eat the healthy lunch mom has prepared.

"How's lunch girls?"

"Delicious!" they both yell!

Siena finishes her plate first and leans over to Kinsley's plate reaching out with her fork. Kinsley puts her hand up in Siena's face.

"Donut, touch my broccoli!"

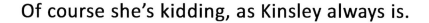

Of course she's kidding, as Kinsley always is.

After sharing their healthy lunch

Mrs. McGrath, asks if the girls are full? Would they like anything else?

Kinsley gets super excited. "Can I have a donut now?"

Siena looks at their mom and says, **"she'll learn one day."**

Recipe for Kinsley's chicken nuggets and broccoli

Nuggets
1 lb or Breast or Thighs
Avocado oil (or ghee butter)

Seasonings
Cut your chicken into 1" cubes
Place into a bowl and toss your favorite seasoning right on top
Siena and Kinsley love just sea salt and garlic powder.
Pre heat to medium/high heat with avocado oil or ghee butter.
Add the chicken to the pan and move it around until all the chicken is a nice crispy golden brown.

Broccoli-
1 Flouret
pre heat over 375f
Cut the Broccoli into as small pieces as you desire
Toss the Broccoli into a bowl, combine a few dashes of sea salt
And a few tbsp. of olive oil. Toss until all oils and salt is dispersed evenly.
Place in an oven safe dish, bake until broccoli is starting to brown. Usually take 10-15 minutes depending on how small you cut the pieces

Honey Mustard Sauce
Combine in a tupperware
½ Cup of Dijon mustard
¼ cup of raw honey
2 tbsp of olive oil

Work Book 1

Circle the Carbohydrates

Circle the Proteins

Work Book 2

(Fill in the blank)

Carbohydrates   **strong**   **Chicken**   **Broccoli**   **donuts**

pizza   **pasta**   **Siena**   **healthy**   **everyday**

Kinsley Loves her _____. Her older sister _Siena_ is trying to
help her learn how to eat
healthy. Siena teaches Kinsley that vegetables are
healThy
that give is energy and fuel to play and have fun. That _carbohydrates_ is
a Protein which helps our muscles grow big
and _strong_. Eating healthy can be fun and adventurous, we
should all try new foods _everyday_.

Nutritional Plate Pie Chart (draw Siena and Kinsley's dish)

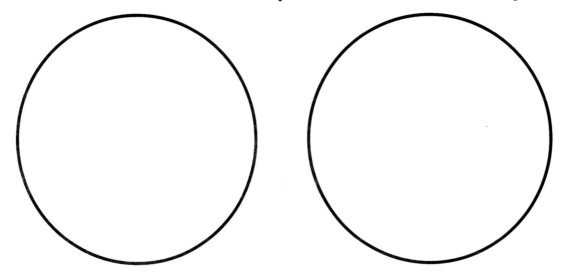

Coloring Page 1

Coloring Page 2